DATE			

2-11

Well Defined

Well Defined
Vocabulary in Rhyme

Michael Salinger

ILLUSTRATIONS BY **Sam Henderson**

WORDSONG
Honesdale, Pennsylvania

To Stephi, for defining love —M.G.S.

Text copyright © 2009 by Michael Salinger
Illustrations copyright © 2009 by Sam Henderson
All rights reserved
Printed in China
Designed by Helen Robinson
First edition
Second printing

Library of Congress Cataloging-in-Publication Data

Salinger, Michael.
Well defined : vocabulary in rhyme / Michael Salinger ; illustrations by Sam Henderson.
p. cm.
ISBN 978-1-59078-615-4 (hardcover : alk. paper)
1. Vocabulary. 2. English language—Rhyme. I. Henderson, Sam. II. Title.
PE1449.S2824 2009
428.1—dc22
2008019101

WORDSONG
An Imprint of Boyds Mills Press, Inc.
815 Church Street
Honesdale, Pennsylvania 18431

CONTENTS

Introduction Say I'm walking down the street, jamming to some tunes popping through my earbuds, when I notice a car slowly cruising up alongside. The driver rolls down the window and shouts something. I pull the earbuds out and motion for the person behind the wheel to repeat what he just said. "I said you look like an erudite man. Could you perhaps help me with some directions?"

Well, what should I do? It all depends on what the word *erudite* means now, doesn't it?

I've always loved words. I guess that is one reason I became a writer. When writing, I spend a hefty chunk of time trying to find just the right word, the one that encapsulates an instant, that provides an image crisp and mountain-spring clear. And when reading someone else's work, I enjoy coming across a word so pithy that it makes me stop in my tracks.

In this book are some amusing poems about a bunch of two-dollar words that may come in handy someday, as well as Sam Henderson's drawings to go with them. I hope you enjoy reading them. I know I had fun writing them. Perhaps you may decide to write a few vocabulary poems of your own—there's no law against it, you know. And who can tell? Increasing your vocabulary just might make you an erudite character. —*M.G.S.*

[**erudite**: possessing great knowledge; learned or scholarly]

Aggregate believes in group hugs

likes large parties, crowds of all sorts

loves a parade

any great grouping whether matched or mixed

will do the trick

when examined in total

because aggregate is the big picture

the whole ball o' wax

the kit and caboodle

all of Grandma's knickknacks

a mass

and/or amassed

[**aggregate:** a collection of objects into a mass]

Berate should hand out earplugs
his lecturing tends to get loud
his criticisms long and severe
he means to demean, that's clear
he tends to go over the top
shouting and scolding with zest
making his victim feel small
is the one thing he does best
needless to say, his friends are far
and few
which just may explain
a thing or two

[**berate:** to scold over a length of time]

Brevity gets right to the point
doesn't dawdle, dicker, or delay
always short and sweet whenever
there is something to do
or say
brevity comes in handy when you
are subject to a chewing out
a bout of the flu
a pain in the neck
or waiting in line for the loo
in fact, this poem has gone on so long
that its recital
would no longer qualify
as an example of its title

[**brevity:** conciseness of expression; shortness]

Capricious doesn't have a lot to do
with logic so
don't spend too much time trying
to figure him or his next move out
'cause he's more likely to act on a whim
than follow any plausible plan
if you had to guess what he would say
or do next
one answer would be admissible:
capricious is
unpredictable

[**capricious:** unpredictable; impulsive]

14 **Circuitous** is one to avoid shortcuts
or any sort of straight line
he's not worried about the most direct route
or trying to save any time
rather he'll soak in the scenery
meander, browse, and digress
taking the path less traveled
eventually he'll get where he's going
though he may be the last to arrive
when asked what took him so long
he'll reply
"It was a lovely day for a drive"

[**circuitous:** having a winding or circular course]

16   **Credulity** doesn't check the facts
        question authority
        or even ask
        if what he's being told is true
        he'll believe any old story
        you care to spin
        not the person to rely on
        when out and about
        mainly because
        it doesn't take too much
        to take him in

[**credulity:** willingness to believe on little evidence]

Diffident doesn't stick out in a crowd
not very gaudy, not very loud
a mixture of shy sprinkled with unsure
what's lacked in confidence
is made up in demure
won't take a chance
a stab
or a shot
the type of reservation
that would not come in handy
when one's on vacation

[**diffident:** hesitant; lacking confidence]

Dilatory avoids direct confrontation
taking his while to wear someone down
his approach is slow and methodical
rather than through he goes around
he'll come at you from the side
at wasting time he is an expert
he doesn't expect a fight when he arrives
he has a different trick up his sleeve
he hopes his actions cause his opponent
to get really bored and leave

[**dilatory:** causing delay; hesitant]

Disingenuous isn't very honest
though she pretends to be utterly sincere
she asks you to judge a book by its cover
while keeping the contents unclear
she'll smile to your face
professing her intention is true
yet all the while aware
that she's full of grade-A baloney
thus, as Holden Caulfield would say,
disingenuous is nothing if not
a phony

[**disingenuous:** insincere; dishonest]

20   **Equivocal** won't make a decision
'cause the facts aren't all in place
the data just doesn't stack up
enough to hazard a guess
between this conclusion
or that
in truth the water's quite muddy
when pressed for opinion
equivocal will answer
"This situation requires
more study"

[**equivocal:** uncertain; confusing]

Erratic never follows a pattern

no set route, rhythm, or road
more of a haphazard approach
stuck in random mode
your guess is as good as mine
as to where he'll end up
or even how he'll get there this time
the only thing about erratic
that can be counted on for sure
is the fact he can't be counted on
this is one bet that's secure

[**erratic:** inconsistent; having no set course]

22   **Exorbitant** is way out of control
knows no reason to act
with moderation, temperance, or restraint
when charging for goods or services
he'll gouge and then declare
that what he asks is fair
even if it's twice
what any bull market
would bear

[**exorbitant:** exceeding appropriate limits]

Extenuating brings a note from his mom

keeps an alibi ready just in case
circumstances beyond his control
form the basis of most all his actions
not to be saddled with blame
he can always find a way to explain
how things just aren't his fault
the result
of this over here
or that over there
now it may sound like an excuse
but chances are
he's telling the truth

[**extenuating:** partially excusing or justifying]

24 **Fiasco** is an utter disaster
if something could go wrong it has
a train off its track
a dam that has burst
a play in which every actor
has forgotten his lines
you would assume that things
couldn't get worse
except the train was carrying poisonous snakes
there was lava behind that dam
and once those actors turn into werewolves
well, you've got a fiasco on your hands

[**fiasco:** total failure]

26 **Florid** is most certainly "all that"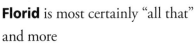
and more
never understated, not one to be demure
a flourish, a flurry, drama's her game
whether writing or speaking her method's the
    same
be big, be flashy, be bold
use curlicues, glitter, and gold
don't hold back
ornamentation trumps content
it's the packaging that matters
when something needs to be sold

[**florid:** ornate; flamboyant]

Gregarious knows how to party
he loves hanging out in a crowd
making friends to him—second nature
always in a group when he goes out
he's happy, he's jovial, and he's friendly
a frat boy who has never grown up
your back-slapping buddy
who's a little too loud
but still too much fun
to rebuff

[**gregarious:** showing enjoyment of the company of others; sociable]

28   **Haphazard** needs neither rhyme nor reason
considering order and pattern
a treasonous act
the fact that her socks don't match
her shirt's inside out
both shoes are for left feet
and her hair sprouts from her head
as if randomly seeded
makes no difference to her
'cause if things are asunder
well then,
she has succeeded

[**haphazard:** random; by chance]

Hypothetical asks the question "what if?"
her comments based on supposition
rather than hard cold facts
not certain to happen thus
anything hypothetical cares to discuss
is founded on theory
so while her remarks may be possible
and sound logical, even legit,
hypothetical has to admit
what she serves for consumption
is totally based on assumption

[**hypothetical:** based on theory or assumption]

30 **Incessant** just doesn't know when to quit
seemingly having no beginning
or end
that dog barking at all hours of the night
that friend who always borrows money
a toothache, an ulcer, bad dreams
the nagging of a parent or spouse
like water torture
incessant accumulates
overflowing the cup
never giving in
never giving up

[**incessant:** unending; ceaseless]

Inevitable is impossible to avoid 31
like some annoying jerk at a party
who has to be dealt with
it's going to happen, you see it coming
no amount of hiding or running
will change this course of destiny
you'll have to accept, one simple fact is
inevitable has a lot in common
with death and taxes

[**inevitable:** unavoidable; certain]

Infiltrate comes uninvited
sneaks in through a side window
or jimmied back door
squeezing through cracks you'd never think
she'd fit
to gather information
or maybe just sit a bit
she's not very flashy
she's not very loud
but she's been known to take notes
while blending in
with the crowd

[**infiltrate:** to gradually enter]

Insidious sneaks under the door

little by little by little
spreads across the floor like morning fog
he'll stick to your shoes
and follow you like a kid brother
who can't be shaken
he's that tickle in the back of your throat
when you absolutely must be quiet
the smell of turpentine
that cheesy song you can't get out of your mind
he's nothing but trouble
but he takes
his time

[**insidious:** sneaky and harmful]

34 **Instigate** likes to get the ball rolling
she's the very first domino to tip
with a word or a deed
instigate will proceed the commencement
of an action
she'll prod, poke, nudge
she'll throw the switch to get things going
in a boat headed for a waterfall
instigate is the one that's
rowing

[**instigate:** to influence or encourage]

Jubilant is beyond plain old happy
she's dancing in the street
kissing strangers, hand-clapping
on cloud nine
whooping to the sky
winning lottery ticket in hand
out of her mind with delight
if you see jubilant you just might,
without being rude,
describe her as being
in a very, very, very
good mood

[**jubilant:** extremely happy; celebrating]

36   **Kudos** loves to give credit
       where credit is due
       when you've done a good job
       he's the one that'll pat you on the back
       you aced that test, won the game
       cut the grass, survived a rabid weasel attack
       he is there with a medal, badge
       maybe a trophy
       to share and point out your glory
       kudos gets my endorsement
       for being the prince
       of positive reinforcement

[**kudos:** praise; approval; recognition]

Lugubrious is, like, *really* sad

and doesn't care who knows it
wailing, crying, moaning
pulling out his hair
anything to show
it's the end of the world as far as he's concerned
some would say his sorrow
is a bit over the top
but lugubrious believes
tears are best handled
with a mop

[**lugubrious:** mournful, sad, or gloomy in an exaggerated way]

38   **Magnanimous** rises above the fray
      never holds a grudge
      is generous in every way
      courageous, noble, and kind
      forgiving for her comes easy
      whether to friend or foe
      she's the kind of person we'd all like to know
      she'll never be petty
      on that you can rely
      magnanimous is a really swell person
      and that ain't no lie

[**magnanimous:** generous in forgetting insults; forgiving]

40   **Martyr** goes down with the ship
      bleeding out vital fluids for his cause
      although while he's being snuffed
      he may expect some applause
      the absence of gratitude, though,
      allows him to let everyone know
      of his sacrifice so unselfish
      for there is one thing
      that martyr finds dreaded
      it's not the suffering he can't take
      it's the fact that he's not getting credit

[**martyr:** hero who suffers; one who suffers to gain sympathy]

Mitigate likes to smooth things over
highlighting reasons for restraint
illuminating circumstances
that may lessen the taint
of an action
so while the ends
may not always justify the means
mitigate asks you consider
a little leniency
in this particular case
'cause the situation
isn't always what it seems

[**mitigate:** make less severe]

42   **Nemesis** lurks round the corner
your name topping her to-do list
ready to pounce and oppose anything
that looks as if it just may go
your way
a cut above your basic enemy
Greek goddess namesake
of divine retribution and vengeance
full of incessant cunning
thus
even though
she's out to get you
you may simply have it
coming

[**nemesis:** opponent or rival who can't be overcome]

Novice hasn't quite figured things out yet
you see he's just been sent into the game
doesn't have much experience
but he's more than willing to try just the same
it's not his fault, everyone has to start
somewhere at sometime
and I'm sure he's gonna
get the hang of things
I'm just saying ...
I'm glad he's your surgeon
and not mine

[**novice:** a beginner in any skill]

44   **Oblivion** I knew him well
      but can't seem to place his face
      I thought he lived here
      but the house is gone
      a smoking hole left in its wake
      in fact, there isn't any hide or hair
      left of old what's-his-name
      could someone please give me a hand—
      what was I looking for
      again?

[**oblivion:** state of being completely forgotten]

46   **Obsolete** is absolutely useless
although in the past
he was reasonably handy
time—it kept on ticking and he
just never bothered to adapt
so now he gets passed over
sits in the corner collecting dust
his colors are fading
his chrome has started to rust
but don't feel too bad for obsolete
his future is not completely bleak
as long as he keeps hanging on
eventually he'll become an antique

[**obsolete:** no longer useful; outmoded]

Pessimism sees the glass half empty

nothing will ever go his way
he won't pet a dog 'cause he's sure it'll bite
won't try skiing, too many broken legs
every cloud is harboring rain
every good deed an ulterior motive
"We're all doomed"
is this guy's rallying cry
no doubt a fairly depressing
way to live one's life
but when one is convinced existence is cursed
it is plainly easier
to always expect the worst

[**pessimism:** tendency to stress negative views]

48   **Petulant** is in no mood
      unless that mood is BAD
      quick to ire, sure to fire
      off remarks quite crude
      always the first to take offense
      petulant's
      prime defense:
      cop a major attitude
      by acting really rude

[**petulant:** unreasonably irritable; crabby]

Pithy gets right to the point
no beating round the bush for her
short and sweet and completely
relevant to the topic at hand
this girl knows what she's talking about
not one to waste words
being concise for her is a snap
this is your go-to gal
when you need a line or a phrase
that cuts through all the crap

[**pithy:** brief and full of meaning]

50 **Quandary** can't decide how to act
seems all of the options are bad
this no-win situation can lead to frustration
damned if ya don't
damned if ya do
there just ain't no good way to choose
might as well
just flip a coin
when caught
in a Catch-22

[**quandary:** state of uncertainty; a dilemma]

Recalcitrant categorically has little use
for any authority
and makes sure everyone knows it
digging in heels, sneering, or
joining a protest
are just a couple ways she'll show it
her chief means of defense
is to defy
the powers that be
by looking at them straight in the eye
and confidently saying
"You're not the boss of me!"

[**recalcitrant:** resisting authority; hard to control]

52 **Recidivism** is incapable of staying out
of trouble
committing crimes, for him, is a habit
he promises virtue
but never succeeds, intends to go straight
but his path always leads
to arrest, trial, incarceration
his anarchistic fixations are categorically chronic
in the garden of humanity
this chap is a weed
but what could you expect
from such a bad seed?

[**recidivism:** repeated or habitual relapse into crime]

Redolent can be an aroma

exuding an odor of some sort
a rose by any other name
smells just as sweet, but just the same
a skunk could make a similar claim
though sometimes not a literal scent
redolent can still give a hint
toward an object's nature
whether fragrance or suggestion
redolent is a description that
comes in handy
whenever one smells a rat

[**redolent:** having or emitting an odor]

54   **Refute** can stop a speaker dead
in her tracks
like a brick wall popping up
out of nowhere
he will halt an argument before
it even begins
no weapons needed when he attacks
because refute comes armed
simply
with the facts

[**refute:** to prove false]

Reiterate—you can say that again! 55
and she will
sometimes rephrased, sometimes verbatim
but the message remains the same
for, you see, reiterate conceives
that once is never enough
to get her message across
it's pretty tough competing
with all the noise of this busy world
so she believes
a notion worth saying
is also worth repeating

[**reiterate:** to say or do again; to repeat]

56 **Resignation** doesn't bother
to put up a fight
speak or stick up for himself
even when he is right
surrender is his usual tactic
resistance is not the game for him
quitting, walking away, throwing hands in the air
are some of his solutions
in fact, the only way for him
to make the situation better
is if his quitting
is done via letter

[**resignation:** the act of giving up or quitting]

Skeptical is not so certain
that what he's being told is the truth
not one to believe the loss of a tooth
will bring in some money
doesn't quite see how his father
walked to school uphill
both ways!
he asks lots of questions
and he's nobody's patsy
pardon me, but
is that a toupee?

[**skeptical:** showing doubt]

58 **Squalid** might be a slob
      if only he cleaned up his act a bit
      his hygiene's the worst
      his housekeeping sucks
      disorder, filth, and disarray are his curse
      living in an open sewer
      would cause fewer visitors to gag
      if cleanliness is next to godliness
      as has been said
      then squalid
      is headed for hell in a handbag

[**squalid**: filthy]

Tacit may not come right out and say

what's on his mind out loud
but a wink or a nod
maybe an eyebrow raised
will allow one to infer
what's going on inside his head
with a fair amount of precision
it's just his way
without saying a word
of offering an agreement
with surreptitious permission

[**tacit:** implied; silently understood]

Transient just can't stay put
whether the grass is greener
or his feet just itch
he's got to be on the move
he likes to switch his location
the way other folks change socks
one can wonder
why he's so consumed by wanderlust
but it's tough to get an answer,
you know,
when the person you'd like to question
is always on the go

[**transient:** indicating a brief stay in a place; momentary]

Transmute isn't afraid of a little change

in fact, he usually makes things better

whether form, appearance,

or nature

there's always something he can tweak

for transmute

a little alteration would never hurt

whether he is referring to

his spiritual constitution

or even the hem of a woman's skirt

[**transmute:** to change from one form to another]

62   **Unctuous** is a little bit slimy
      kinda smooth, a little greasy
      slippery in appearance or texture
      and sometimes deed
      unctuous would have you deem
      that she is made of silk
      if she's talking about her dress
      well, with that I may agree
      but if she means the sincerity
      of all the things she says
      well, that I find a little hard to believe

[**unctuous:** insincere; oily]

Verbose always has something to say
and say and say and say
when one word would do
verbose uses two
or three or four or five or six ...
one of his favorite tricks
is to just keep prattling on and on
giving his listeners absolutely no choice
because even more than words
verbose is in love with the sound
of his own voice

[**verbose:** using or containing too many words]

Wistful likes to dwell on thoughts
especially if the notion is a little bit sad
he has a permanent boo-boo lip
but on him it doesn't look bad
you will find him musing
if not amusing
but don't you fret
during his times of distress
or if there's a tear in his eye
for wistful is only really happy
when he feels like
he's going to cry

[**wistful:** sad; longing]